# Blind Martha

*Spreading sunshine in darkness*

**CHRISTIAN LIGHT PUBLICATIONS INC.**
P.O. BOX 1212
Harrisonburg, Virginia 22803-1212
(540) 434-0768

ISBN: 978-1-943929-90-0

Cover design and layout: Kristi Yoder

Second printing: November 2017

Printed in China

*Published by:*
TGS International
P.O. Box 355
Berlin, Ohio 44610 USA
Phone: 330-893-4828
Fax: 330-893-2305
www.tgsinternational.com

TGS001570

# Blind Martha

*Spreading sunshine
in darkness*

*Velina Showalter*

Illustrated by Shirley Myers

Akron sprawls over a hill like an ordinary town in Pennsylvania. On the side of the hill on Eleventh Street, a small brick house clings to the slope. Flowers around the house add a splash of color to the well-groomed yard.

Clean laundry flaps on the line, waving a
cheerful welcome to those passing by. This is
the home of Martha and her dog Jodie.

Martha was only two years old when the doctor told her mother, "Mrs. Hoover, your daughter has Coats' disease. It is very rare. Someday she will be blind."

Martha clung to her mother. *What is he saying?* she wondered, her brown eyes troubled. She couldn't understand the doctor's English, since she spoke only Pennsylvania Dutch.

Martha soon forgot her fears over the doctor's words. A few years passed. She played happily with her brothers and sisters on the farm. They tumbled in the hay, picked flowers in the meadow, and played with newborn kittens.

One day Martha buried her nose in a daisy to see the detail of the petals. When she tipped her head sideways to focus on it, her mother said, "I think Martha can see with only one eye!" Martha's mother took her to the doctor for a checkup shortly before Martha began first grade.

"Martha is blind in one eye," the doctor confirmed. "And her vision is very low in the other."

In school, Martha hunched over her desk and pushed her thick glasses to the top of her nose. Carefully she traced around the letters. *This is hard!* she thought. *If only I could see the blackboard.* Day after day at the little country school, Martha's teacher Anna Mae watched her struggle. Finally Anna Mae said, "Martha needs too much help. She ought to attend a special school."

So Martha began riding the bus to Farmersville School. Tears rolled down her cheeks when she looked around her new classroom. It was full of children with special needs. Martha thought, *My mind still works! I don't understand why I should be here.*

After a few years at the public school, she returned to the little country school. As she biked to school with her brothers and sisters, she thought happily, *This is where I belong.*

But school was a struggle for Martha. When she was in sixth grade, her teacher Anna Mae watched Martha hold her book close to her eyes. "Give this a try," said Anna Mae, handing her a magnifying glass. Some days later she sat down beside Martha, a look of compassion on her face. "This year I have only fourteen students, so I have time to teach you Braille."

Martha's fingers slipped across the rows of raised dots. Braille was a whole new language for her. But after much practice, Martha sighed, "I still depend more on sight than on my fingers." She would not completely master Braille until later in life.

Martha enjoyed working outside more than sitting at a desk in school. Her father patiently showed her how to feed the pigs and gather the eggs. She cleaned out stables and drove the tractor. But her favorite summer job was working in the hayfield, stacking bales on the wagon.

One day when Martha was twelve, she heard the familiar hum of the sewing machine as her sister sewed a new dress. "May I please sew something?" she begged her mother.

"I'm sorry, Martha. I don't think you can see well enough to sew." Martha turned away to hide her tears.

Several weeks later, Martha's mother went away for the day. Martha rummaged through the attic until she found a piece of fabric. *I could make a pillow out of this*, she thought. Happily she snipped and sewed. When she heard her mother coming in the door, she ran to meet her.

"Look at what I sewed, Mom!" Her fingers trembled with excitement as she held out the pillow for her mother to examine.

"That's beautiful, Martha! Why, I believe you can learn to sew dresses." And she did.

After completing eight years of school, Martha told her mother, "I want a job like the rest of my friends." In her community it was common for Mennonite children to stop school after eighth grade.

"Maybe my cousin Rachel could use some help," her mother said. "She has four young children. Let's go see what she says."

"What can you do for me?" asked Rachel. "I've been looking for a maid."

"I can sew, clean, cook, bake, and take care of children," Martha replied.

Despite her limitations, Martha worked hard. She helped Rachel and her family for four years. "You're a good worker, Martha!" Rachel would say. Martha just smiled.

Several years later, Martha got a job twisting pretzels by hand at Martin's Pretzel Bakery in Akron. She loved her new job. Her fingers flew as she rolled the pretzel dough into long, thin logs. With a quick jerk of her wrists, she twisted the logs into a pretzel shape, pressing down the ends.

One evening Martha was biking home from the bakery when her bike wheel ran off the edge of the road. Her bike flipped, and she fell facedown on the pavement. Groaning, she picked herself up and examined her glasses. "Oh, no!" she said. Her glasses were badly scuffed. Then, though her knees were torn and bleeding, she determinedly mounted her bike and pedaled toward home. *I see a black dot, and it's getting bigger and bigger.* Her heart thudded with worry.

As soon as she came home, she grabbed the phone. "Hello, may I speak to Dr. Naize?" When she described her problem to the eye doctor, he told her to come to his office the next day.

The purring of the milking pump woke Martha the next morning. *It must be morning,* she thought, *because my family is doing chores. Why is it still dark?* Suddenly she understood. *I can't see at all! No!* She wanted to scream. Big, salty tears rolled down her cheeks and onto the pillow. She lay there for a long time.

Then Martha remembered a verse she had read in the Bible. "I will never leave thee, nor forsake thee." God was with her! Another verse came to her mind: "My help cometh from the LORD." *God will help me,* she thought. She sat up, swung her legs over the edge of the bed, groped across the room, and got dressed for the day.

Quietly the family ate their breakfast, realizing Martha had a serious problem. They were relieved to see Martha leave for the eye doctor.

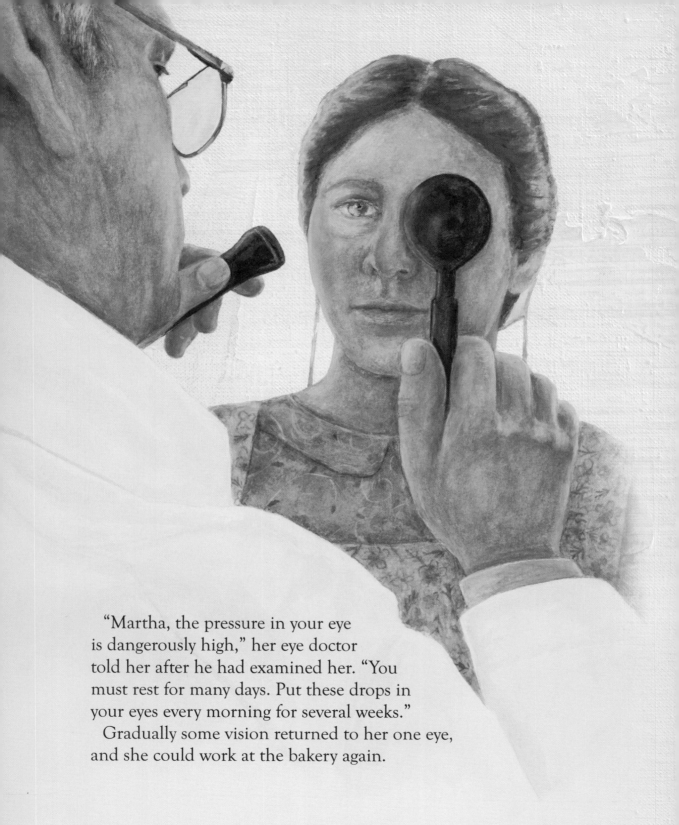

"Martha, the pressure in your eye
is dangerously high," her eye doctor
told her after he had examined her. "You
must rest for many days. Put these drops in
your eyes every morning for several weeks."
    Gradually some vision returned to her one eye,
and she could work at the bakery again.

"I don't know what to do," Martha told her sister Ella one day. "I can't see well enough to bike to work anymore, and it's unhandy to always hire a driver."

"I know what you mean." Ella had vision problems too. "Why don't we see if we can rent that mobile home close to the bakery?"

After they had moved, the two sisters were walking along the country road one day. "I enjoy walking to work," Martha told her sister. "I feel refreshed when I hear the birds sing, and I love to breathe in the fresh morning air."

That summer, Martha told her friend Alta, "I've been having more eye problems lately. Sometimes everything is dark. Then after a while some vision comes back."

"Wow, that must be hard," said Alta. "I'm so sorry."

"It is hard. When I can see a little, I really notice the pretty flowers, the green grass, and the blue sky. I pray that the Lord will take care of me and that His will would be done, but I do tell the Lord that I need to see!"

Then Martha sighed as she said, "I feel it is God's will for me to be blind."

When Martha was twenty-eight, her eye doctor told her, "Martha, there's a chance that laser surgery will help your eyes."

Martha bowed her head and slowly said, "I will pray and ask God for direction."

She decided to have the surgery. The morning after the operation, the doctor shone a bright flashlight into her eyes. "Can you see this?" he asked hopefully. Martha stared into total darkness. Once again she turned to God for strength to humbly accept total blindness.

For Martha, the sun had gone down, never to rise again. She could no longer see the difference between day and night. She had to depend on her memory to envision color. To know who people were, she now had to listen to the sound of their voices. She had to begin using her fingers to feel her surroundings. Her world had become a dark, dark night without any moon or stars.

Since she could no longer see at all, Martha quit her job at the pretzel factory. She and her sister Ella went to VisionCorps in Lancaster to look for work.

"What can you do? Shall we teach you how to cook and clean?" asked the lady behind the desk.

"Oh, no," Martha laughed. "I can cook, clean, and sew. I take care of myself!"

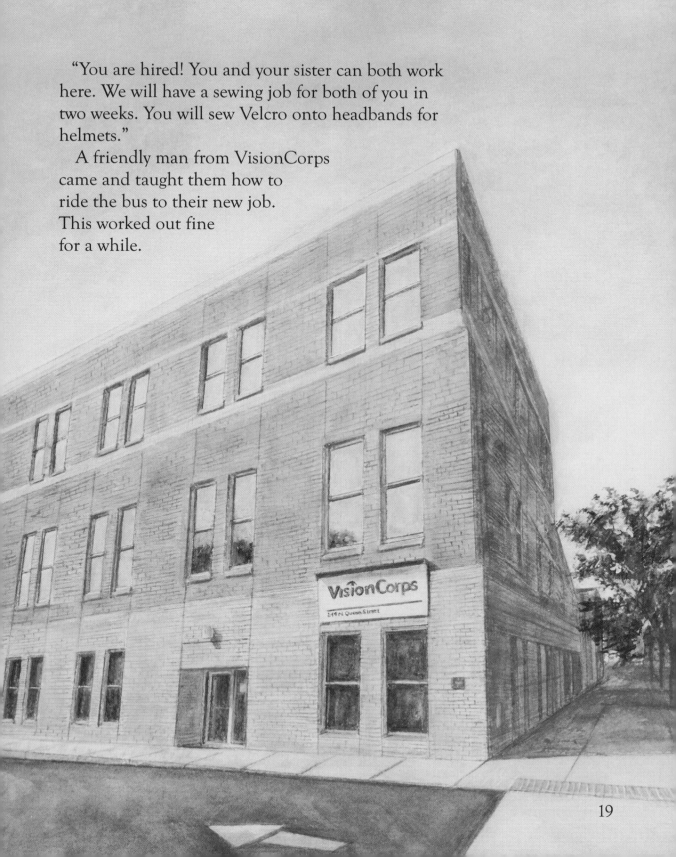

"You are hired! You and your sister can both work here. We will have a sewing job for both of you in two weeks. You will sew Velcro onto headbands for helmets."

A friendly man from VisionCorps came and taught them how to ride the bus to their new job. This worked out fine for a while.

VisionCorps

One day Pete Horn, one of the staff members at VisionCorps, said, "Martha, you should use a white cane."

"No, I do not want a white cane. I would rather have a guide dog."

"If you learn to use the cane, we will help you get a dog."

"That's a deal!"

So Martha learned to use the cane, but she never learned to like it. She was walking down the sidewalk one day, using her cane to find her way, when her cane bumped into something. Whatever it was, it didn't feel hard like a light pole.

"Watch where you are going!" a woman yelled angrily. Martha apologized, but the woman was still upset that Martha had hit her leg.

Later, Martha explained to Pete Horn why she didn't like the cane. "It's a cold, lifeless stick that lets you run into tree branches or out into the street in places where the curb slopes and blends into the street. That's why I want a dog."

So Martha filled out papers to apply for a guide dog. Finally she got a phone call from The Seeing Eye, Incorporated, in Morristown, New Jersey. "Martha, we're ready for you to come be matched up with a Seeing Eye dog. Come prepared to be in training for one month."

Martha could hardly speak. At last, her dream had come true!

Within a few weeks' time, she made the three-hour trip to The Seeing Eye in New Jersey. A guide named Joan showed her all around the premises and introduced her to the other students and instructors. Then Joan took Martha to her room, where she would board for a month. Martha's heart skipped a beat when she discovered a dog chain in her room. *Having a dog will change my life dramatically,* she thought. *Finally I'll be able to be more independent.*

The days passed in a blur of activity and instructions. Martha had to walk with the instructors before they could match a dog with her stride. Martha wanted a dog that would walk fast and pull on the harness.

With tears of gratitude, she accepted her first dog, Tessie, a golden retriever. But learning to work together was a process that took several weeks. Martha walked many blocks in the city with Tessie. "I'm getting tired of this!" she sighed after a long day of practice. "But we'll keep going, won't we, Tessie?" She stroked the dog's silky head.

Together they learned how to walk into unknown territory, find their way in and out of buildings, stay on schedule, and meet strangers. Martha had to learn how to take care of her dog, and her dog had to learn how to be responsible for her. Slowly Martha grew confident that Tessie would guide her safely. But the big test still lay ahead—New York City.

What a noisy place it was! The sounds of moving vehicles, screeching brakes, and honking horns in New York City overwhelmed Martha. The sidewalk was jammed with people, dogs, and baby strollers. Tessie made her way to the right and to the left, sticking her nose between people. Martha felt the crowd open as she came striding behind her dog. *What if I run into someone?* thought Martha. *No, I've got to stop worrying. I need to trust Tessie.* She relaxed her grip on the harness and let Tessie lead the way. Together they marched through the crowds, explored a department store, rode escalators inside a huge building, and ate in a restaurant. They found their way through subway stations and visited Times Square.

At the end of the day, the instructor told Martha, "You followed your dog very well."

"I had no other choice!" Martha gave a sigh of relief. They had passed the test!

23

"Look here," Martha said to Tessie when she brought her home. "We are going to put your bed in my room. Your dish will be right here beside the door." Martha talked a lot to Tessie, and they became good friends.

Martha faced new challenges when her sister Ella got married and moved away. Now Martha was living in the mobile home alone. She had to walk a mile every morning and evening to and from the bus stop.

"I know what I want to do," she said to herself. "I'm going to buy a house!"

After some time, Martha bought the little red brick house on Eleventh Street. She couldn't see the beautiful view from her window or the green yard that sloped to the road, but when all her belongings were moved in, she was the happiest lady in town!

Twenty years have passed since the sun went down in Martha's world. After working for her for four years, Tessie was replaced by Arty. Then Jodie, a small black lab, came into her home.

Jodie and Martha work together as a team. As soon as Martha adjusts the harness on Jodie's back, Jodie takes the full responsibility of a serious working dog. When Martha is ready to go shopping, she secures a backpack on her own back and says, "Forward. Door." At the end of the sidewalk she says, "Right." Then they stride along.

Jodie carefully leads Martha around electric poles, up and down curbs, and over rough spots or other obstacles. Martha decides when to cross the street. She listens for traffic to know when it is safe to cross. She keeps track of where they are and where they are going. She listens to sounds echoing off the buildings as she walks. All her senses are very keen—except her sight. She can feel when Jodie steps up or down, or goes around an obstacle. Jodie chooses the path, and Martha follows very closely.

At one of the crossings in Akron, a special sign has been posted that says, "Blind Pedestrian Crossing." This helps drivers look out for Martha.

When Martha comes to the traffic light, she asks Jodie, "Where is the button?" Jodie walks to the pole and points her nose at the "walk" button, and Martha presses the button.

When they hear a signal like a bird chirping, they cross the street together. "Good dog, Jodie," Martha says.

31

Martha knows the grocery store like her own house. She finds the items on her list and slips them into her backpack, keeping one hand on Jodie's harness. Jodie knows her way around the store too. She pulls on the harness when she sees the dog food aisle. At the checkout, the clerk is happy to meet them. "Is it okay if I give Jodie a treat?" she asks. She knows these dogs are allowed to eat only what their masters approve.

"Oh, yes!" Martha laughs. "Jodie would never forgive me if I would say no!" Then Martha carefully pulls her money from her purse. Each kind of bill has its own special compartment.

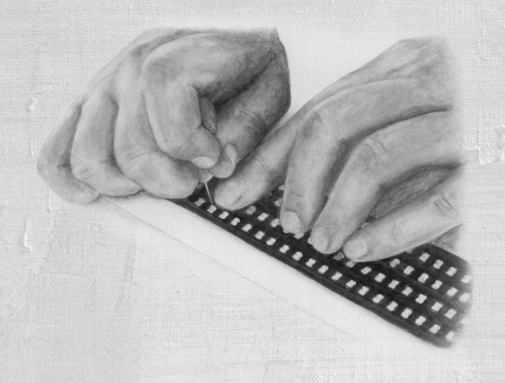

After Martha comes home, she puts the groceries away. She removes Jodie's harness, and Jodie plops on the spare bed for a nap.

The phone rings and Martha says, "Hello! This is Martha and Jodie."

Jodie pricks up her ears and listens. After Martha hangs up the phone, she explains, "Jodie, tomorrow we will go to town with Brenda. We will go shopping for dress fabric."

When they arrive at the store the next day, her friend Brenda describes the fabric to Martha so she can decide what to buy. When Martha gets home, she uses a stylus to write Braille notes to clip to the fabric. "This helps me remember what color I bought," she explains to Brenda.

After she sews a new dress, she pins a small plastic button to it to color code her dress before hanging it in the closet. The button is taken from an organized box that holds buttons of all shapes. Martha says, "When there is a funeral, I want to be sure to wear a black dress!"

One day Brenda looked at Martha when she came out wearing a new dress. "Martha," she said kindly, "your sleeve is sewn on inside out."

"Oh!" Martha laughed, turning to go back inside to change. "It looks like I'll have to use a seam ripper!"

When Martha goes to work at VisionCorps, Jodie rides along on the bus. After Martha clocks in, Jodie lies on a mat by her feet. She plays with her favorite squeaky toy while Martha assembles parts for helmets and packs them into boxes. Martha and the other blind workers laugh and talk as they work.

Martha's workday ends at three o'clock.
Before she walks to the bus station, she
fills a plastic bag with water at the fountain
for Jodie's drink.

After riding home on the bus,
Martha has time to relax.

37

Often Martha does extra sewing or baking for other people. She enjoys crocheting or listening to audiobooks. Martha prefers to listen to an audio Bible rather than reading the many bulky volumes of her Braille Bible, which fill several boxes.

On Sunday mornings, Martha goes to Conestoga Old Order Mennonite Church. Often Mary Shirk, a friend who has a horse and buggy, stops by to give Martha and Jodie a ride.

They arrive at the white frame church, and Martha finds her place on the wooden bench. Jodie relaxes by her feet, and Martha joins in the singing. She listens attentively to the preacher. When they kneel to pray, Martha has many things to thank the Lord for. She thanks God for blessing her with friends, and most of all, for Jesus! He promised to never leave her or forsake her.

*Clip clop, clip clop.* Church is over, and
Martha, Jodie, and Mary ride in the
carriage as the horse slowly climbs the hill
to the little house on Eleventh Street.

They drive past all the familiar places—
the little country school she had attended,
the farm where Martha grew up with her
brothers and sisters, and the pond where
she used to swim with her cousins.

41

All around Martha are beautiful things she cannot see—the green grass, the sky, and the light of the sun. But Martha's life is full of light because she walks with God. She spreads sunshine wherever she goes. Her neighbors know her as a person who lives to give and does not complain.

She has many friends. She tells them, "You know, becoming blind has helped me see what is most important in life. The most important thing is not sight, but living for God who is the true Light."

# About the Author

Velina Showalter was born in 1952 and raised in an Old Order Mennonite home in Ontario, Canada. She taught school for twenty years, the last seven of which were in Farmington, New Mexico. There she married John Showalter, a widower who had five children, in 1989. Three more children were added to the family by this union. After four years in New Mexico, the family moved to Grand Junction, Colorado, where they lived for ten years before moving to their current residence near Greencastle, Pennsylvania. Velina and her husband are members of the Paradise Mennonite Church in Washington County, Maryland.

Velina loves the Lord and the work of His kingdom. She works part-time at Friendly Village, a church school for special-needs children. Writing is her hobby and a way to bless others. She is the author of *Amanda Mussleman* and *Four Angels*, both published by CAM.

Researching to write biographies has given her enjoyable interviews with source persons and rewarding times in historical libraries. Children as well as adults can benefit from Velina's efforts to bring to life outstanding persons in our Anabaptist heritage.

You can contact Velina by writing to her in care of Christian Aid Ministries, P.O. Box 360, Berlin, Ohio 44610.

# About the Illustrator

Shirley Myers is a freelance artist who resides at Roth's Farm Village, located in Spring Grove, Pennsylvania. There in her studio she paints, using her preferred medium, designer's gouache. Nature scenes and animals are among her favorite subject matter. She also has a love and fascination for life-like or hyper-realistic portraiture that has been sketched or painted by other artists.

Besides painting, Shirley enjoys writing prose and poetry, reading, and spending time with her friends.

# Christian Aid Ministries

Christian Aid Ministries was founded in 1981 as a nonprofit, tax-exempt 501(c)(3) organization. Its primary purpose is to provide a trustworthy and efficient channel for Amish, Mennonite, and other conservative Anabaptist groups and individuals to minister to physical and spiritual needs around the world. This is in response to the command to ". . . do good unto all men, especially unto them who are of the household of faith" (Galatians 6:10).

Each year, CAM supporters provide approximately 15 million pounds of food, clothing, medicines, seeds, Bibles, Bible story books, and other Christian literature for needy people. Most of the aid goes to orphans and Christian families. Supporters' funds also help to clean up and rebuild for natural disaster victims, put up Gospel billboards in the U.S., support several church-planting efforts, operate two medical clinics, and provide resources for needy families to make their own living. CAM's main purposes for providing aid are to help and encourage God's people and bring the Gospel to a lost and dying world.

CAM has staff, warehouses, and distribution networks in Romania, Moldova, Ukraine, Haiti, Nicaragua, Liberia, Israel, and Kenya. Aside from management, supervisory personnel, and bookkeeping operations, volunteers do most of the work at CAM locations. Each year, volunteers at our warehouses, field bases, Disaster Response Services projects, and other locations donate over 200,000 hours of work.

CAM's ultimate purpose is to glorify God and help enlarge His kingdom. ". . . whatsoever ye do, do all to the glory of God" (1 Corinthians 10:31).

# The Way to God and Peace

We live in a world contaminated by sin. Sin is anything that goes against God's holy standards. When we do not follow the guidelines that God our Creator gave us, we are guilty of sin. Sin separates us from God, the source of life.

Since the time when the first man and woman, Adam and Eve, sinned in the Garden of Eden, sin has been universal. The Bible says that we all have "sinned and come short of the glory of God" (Romans 3:23). It also says that the natural consequence for that sin is eternal death, or punishment in an eternal hell: "Then when lust hath conceived, it bringeth forth sin: and sin, when it is finished, bringeth forth death" (James 1:15).

But we do not have to suffer eternal death in hell. God provided forgiveness for our sins through the death of His only Son, Jesus Christ. Because Jesus was perfect and without sin, He could die in our place. "For God so loved the world that he gave his only begotten Son, that whosoever believeth in him should not perish, but have everlasting life" (John 3:16).

A sacrifice is something given to benefit someone else. It costs the giver greatly. Jesus was God's sacrifice. Jesus' death takes away the penalty of sin for everyone who accepts this sacrifice and truly repents of their sins. To repent of sins means to be truly sorry for and turn away from the things we have done that have violated God's standards (Acts 2:38; 3:19).

Jesus died, but He did not remain dead. After three days, God's Spirit miraculously raised Him to life again. God's Spirit does something similar in us. When we receive Jesus as our sacrifice and repent of our sins, our hearts are changed. We become spiritually alive! We develop new desires and attitudes (2 Corinthians 5:17). We begin to make choices that please God (1 John 3:9). If we do fail and commit sins, we can ask God for forgiveness. "If we confess our sins, he is faithful and just to forgive us our sins, and to cleanse us from all unrighteousness" (1 John 1:9).

Once our hearts have been changed, we want to continue growing spiritually. We will be happy to let Jesus be the Master of our lives and will want to become more like Him. To do this, we must meditate on God's Word and commune with God in prayer. We will testify to others of this change by being baptized and sharing the good news of God's victory over sin and death. Fellowship with a faithful group of believers will strengthen our walk with God (1 John 1:7).